MW01658043

The BOOK of MARQUE

by

Marque Frazier

This book is published by
Avante Garde Productions
1378 Harry Street
Ypsilanti, Michign 48198

DESIGNED BY MARQUE FRAZIER
for
Avante Garde Productions

Frazier, Marque E.
The BOOK of MARQUE.
1, Poems. 2, Lyrics. 3, African-American Literature. 4, Autobiography. I Title

Library of Congress Cataloging-in-Publication Data 99-091239

ISBN 0-9674950-9-1

Art by Marque

All Photos by AVG. PRODUCTIONS

This book is dedicated to the spirit of "Loving Thyself... First"

And to the memory of

My Grandmother,
Mattie Frazier.

Cousin,
Tony Frazier.

My two, other, fathers,
Geno Alexander and Zebulon Long.

Acknowledgments

Thank you Universe, God, Allah, Buddah, Jesus, Jehovah and all the Powers that be.

My parents
Betty Frazier and Roosevelt Flowers for their love, support and 'some good ass' DNA.

My little brother (one of 14 brothers and sisters)
Samuel Alexander, my biggest fan.

My nieces
Sharday and Brittany Alexander
Their mom
Mia Alexander-Darwin

My Soul Mate
Charles Coleman, the inspiration for the "Natural Phenomenon" chapter.
Thank You.

My cousins
Evelyn Jordan, Lavelle Van Horn, Greg 'Sergio' Cooper, Gary and Tammi Herndon, Lakrecia Herndon, Corey Herndon, Michael Herdon, Roderick Sullivan, Vance Mead, Cornelius Mead, Milton Mead and the Mead family, Denny Frazier, Sharron Frazier, CC Frazier, Daniel Frazier Jr., Marcy Higdon, Roz and Omar Shabazz, Alvin "Pete" Gray, Thomas and LaTasha Page Jr., Autumn Frazier, Tracey "Imani" Washington-Howard & the Gang, Katrina, Charles Ray, Ron, Darryl "Scoot", Renee, Jalina, Kiora, Erica

My Uncles and Aunts
Mary and Charles Herndon, Willie Cee Higdon, James Frazier, Lee and Pam Frazier, Daniel and Evelyn Frazier, Cleveland and Carmen Washington, Lunell Harden, Horace Frazier Jr., Brenda Frazier-Page-Towns, Thomas Page Sr. Barabara and Chester Van Horn,
Agnes and Joseph Jackson, Shirley Jackson, Dollie Henson, Cheryl Frazier, Aunt Helen and Uncle Bud,

My Grandfather and idol,
Horace Frazier Sr.

My Peoples
Margaret Flowers and sisters -Gia Flowers, Tammy, Bre'ana, Rhonda, Donna, Tina, Brenda, Denise, Bridget, Renee, Pinky, brothers Darryl and Tyrone
Steve Dishman, Richard Judge, Kerwin Watkins, Jeffery Redmond, James Thorpe, Stanley Demoss, Chris Pink and the late Bobbie Davenport, Billie Davenport, Timothy Smith, Gloria Campbell (the baby's mama), Delfonzo Harris, Dykema Richardson, James Brown and Lannie Myles, Janice Marshall (the other baby's mama), Theodore Pool, Arnold Andrew Kelley, Jerome Williams, Jerome Jackson, Jerome Taylor and family, The Grays, The Minors, William James, Andrew Hine (London),
The Flight Attendants of Northwest Airlines (thanks for all of the jumpseat therapy sessions)

Shibuya, Japan 1999

Contents

1. Black World

2. Natural Phenomenon

3. Drama

4. In Between

5. No Love

6. Oooh...Aaah..!

7. Interview With Jesus

And God said, "Let there be..."

Marque *(mark);*

to make an impression;
a recognized standard of quality;
to take note;
one of a kind;
like no other.

"We are... an insecure world... trying to see itself."
-marque

CHAPTER ONE

Black World

Black World

Welcome to Black World where we don't use money.
You can have anything you want beause all material things are free.
In Black World there is no sickness and disease.
No greed.
No hunger.
No poverty.
In Black World even the Pope is black.
As a matter of fact,
they had to re check that.
A Black woman became the President.
Passed a law.
Housing for all.
No rent.
They serve soul food on planes
with Kool-aid and Tang.
You never have to stand in line
and everything starts on time.

Welcome to Black World.
It's an easy place to live.
Everyone is welcome .
We're only here to give.

Welcome to Black World
where there is no crime.
No security systems.
No relatives doing time.
All your groceries are free
and there are no commercials on TV.
Everyone in Black World has good credit.
Because
we don't ask
and we don't check.
In Black World there are no plantations of the mind
and we have cures for pain and dying.
Black World is almost a perfect place
but even here exists an evil race.
Created really just to keep the balance.
It will seek and destroy at any opportune chance.
In Black World all your dreams do come true.
You can have the desires of your heart.
You can even take vacations on the moon.

Welcome to Black World.
It's an easy place to live.
Everyone is welcome and
we have plenty of everything to give.

Anybody wanna go?

Samuel Alexander
"brother"

Betty Frazier

My Mom

My 33rd Birthday

Got a call from my mom today.
Just called to say
Happy Birthday.
We talked about spiritual and worldly things,
Human needs,
Our family.

She took me back to the day I was born
and how she was so young.
Talked of how she didn't know what to do.
"Child... your grandmomma and aunts... mostly raised you."
"They were all part of that village
and by myself
I could'nt have done it."

"Mom did it hurt?"
"Naw, they cut you out."
"You were upside down
and coming feet first."
I told her I wanted to save the world.
As only a mother would say,
she said, "Yeah babe.
You will...I'm sure."

Got another birthday call.
This time from my little brother.
He's one of a kind, sensitive and like no other.
He said, "Boy you getting old"
"Well, you're right behind me."
"But I look young I'm told
and my life is stress free."
We talked about giving respect
and how much we both... get.
'Specially from the new and young set.
Now we're the ones older than the rest.
We reminisced on our childhood.
The love, the fun and just how good it was.
My little brother.
Still trying to find his own way.
It was a real good birthday.
That February on
the 20th day.

My Mom

My mom is way more than just a mother.
She's my Alpha and Omega.
Out of her darkness and into the light.
My first breath.
My first sight.

It's a love connection
From high above.
Mother and son.
An overwhelming love.

The mom that always told the truth
about life and living.
And that Santa Claus was you.

The one I'd do anything for
And she would for me.
My only best friend.
The only one who truly understands me.

My girl.
The one.
My mom.
She truly is
An awesome phenomenon.

Auntie Mama

MY AUNTIE MAMA IS MY MOMS' SISTER.
SHE BASICALLY RAISED ME.
SHE TAUGHT ME HOW TO TIE MY SHOES,
TELL TIME
AND MADE MY FIRST GINGERBREAD COOKIE.
"REMEMBER AUNTIE?"
SHE HAS ALWAYS BEEN GOOD TO ME.
MY NUMBER ONE FAN.
AND MY AUNTIE CAN COOK LIKE NOBODY CAN.
"IT'S GOOD Y'ALL."

AS A TEEN I WENT TO LIVE WITH HER.
MY FIRST TASTE OF FREEDOM , I THOUGHT.
SHE TAUGHT ME HOW TO DRIVE A 5-SPEED CAR
BUT Y'ALL SHOULD HAVE SEEN HOW WE FOUGHT.
"WHERE YOU GOING BOY?"
"AND WHO YOU GOING WITH?"
"WHY IS SHE QUESTIONING ME LIKE THIS?"

SHE IS THE FUNNIEST WOMAN I KNOW.
MY AUNTIE ALWAYS STEALS THE SHOW.

SHE LOVED ME LIKE HER OWN SON
AND FROM THE HEART THIS COMES.
I AM WHO I AM TODAY,
BECAUSE,
THIS DAY YOU WERE BORN.

I LOVE YOU AUNT BARB.

YOU'RE A SUPERSTAR.

3-Jan 96

BLACK MALE BARBIE

HE HAS THE BARBIE DOLL JEEP.
ALL THE BARBIE DOLL CLOTHES.
THE BARBIE DOLL HOUSE
AND
THE BARBIE CELL PHONE.

HE FLYS BARBIE DREAMJETS.
THE BOEINGS AND JUMBOS.
NONSTOP TO ANYWHERE AND THEN
FIRST CLASS ONLY.

HE'S LIVED IN LOS ANGELES
SAN FRANCISCO
NEW YORK AND CHICAGO.

SHOPS IN
LONDON
PARIS
AND TOKYO.

CHAMPAGNE, CAVIAR, SUSHI AND PATE
MARRIOTS, RADDISONS AND HYATTS
HE HAS STAYED.

LIMOS AND MEMOS
SOIREES AND DATES.
ALL THE ACCESSORIES.
NOW HE NEEDS A MATE.

"mother and brother"

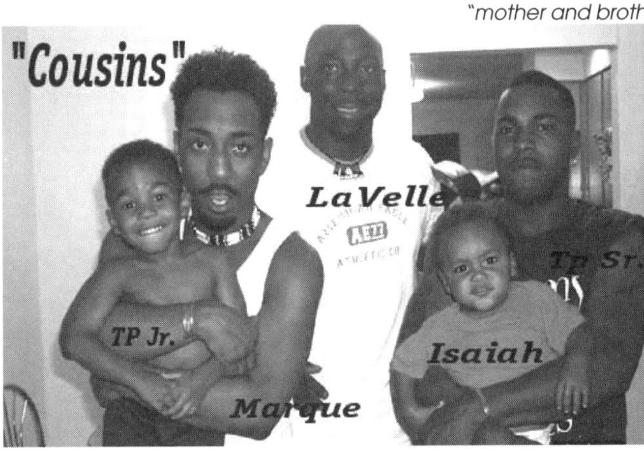

WHAT I AM

I HAVE MY GRANDFATHERS' HAIR

AND I HAVE MY GRANDMOTHERS' EYES.

MY DADS' LIPS AND NOSE

AND MY MOMS' STYLE AND FLAIR.

MY DADS' COOL .

MY MOMS' MOVES.

CHARISMA LIKE MY UNCLE

AND DRAMA LIKE MY AUNT.

I AM THE BOY VERSION OF MY GIRL COUSIN.

I'M A BIG BROTHER AND

A LITTLE BROTHER TOO.

A SON

A GRANDSON

A NEPHEW .

AN UNLCLE

A FRIEND AND

A COUSIN TOO.

I AM

A SPIRITUAL AND PHYSICAL

SORT OF EVERYMAN.

THIS IS WHAT I TRULY AM .

I DEFINE ME

This is my world
and you're more than welcome to visit.
I've checked out your world.
Ain't trying to land on that planet.

I'm the star of this video
and you're just the co-star.
How you gon' produce,
direct
and star
in my video?
Who do you think you are?

I defines me.
It's about what I see.
It was destiny.
The way it was s'ppose to be.
This is my movie.

I defines who I am.
Not no woman nor no man.
Cause this is my life.
And it's my time.
I know what works for me.
This is my DVD.

I am who I am.
I can't change that.
Nor would I allow you
to cloud where I'm at.
This is the video that I produced.
This is my world.
This is my planet.

CLARK BATCHELOR

CLARK BATCHELOR WAS A
STUDENT
A PRETTY BOY
AND A FLIGHT ATTENDANT.
HAD IT GOING ON
AND DID NOT REALLY FIT IN.
HE WAS OLDER THAN US AND STAYED ACROSS THE HALL FROM RUSS.
HE HAD THE HAIR THE FACE AND THE FASHIONS.
WE ALL WONDERED WHERE HE WAS FROM.

LAID OFF FOR
A WHILE.
THOUGHT HE'D CHANGE HIS LIFESTYLE.
DID WHAT HE HAD TO DO
SO HE CAME TO HOWARD U.

"BUT YOU USED TO FLY
AND GOT TO GET AWAY," I'D SAY.
"IF I WERE YOU,
I KNOW I COULDN'T STAY.
SO HOOK ME UP.
I'LL TRADE."

HE SAID, "FLYING... IT WAS OK."
THE DAYS OFF... THE LIFESTYLE... AND THE PAY.
THE DESTINATIONS AND THE PASSES.
I'M LIKE
"FUCK SCHOOL AND ALL
THESE CLASSES."
CAN I START RIGHT AWAY?
ARE THEY HIRING TODAY?

FIFTEEN YEARS HAVE GONE BY SINCE I STARTED TO FLY.
I CAN'T SEE WHY CLARK LEFT THE SKY.
IN ME HE INSPIRIED AND I WILL NEVER GET TIRED
OF THE SKY AND THE MIRACLE OF FLYING.

Come With Me

Come with me to eternity
With the victory of unity.
A world to see
Where humanity
Is free to see reality.

Free of fear.
Free of hate.
Full of love.
Don't be late.

This place I know.
For all to go.
No cargo.
Leave all baggage at home.

No more heartache and pain.
Agony and shame.
No one else to blame.
Don't have to play old games.

It's our destiny.
Our true journey.
To see and be.
All we can be.

All your dreams can come true.
All you need to do
Is fall in love ...
..with you.

LaVelle & Marque
Flt. From CLE
Janet Jackson Concert
7/12/98

COUSINS

Your mamas' sisters' kids
and
Your uncles' kids too.
Your play aunts' three
'cause they grew up with you.
The one you used to pretend
but really was your good friend.
The one that married in
that you still considered kin.

The first ones and second ones
and those you never heard of.
The one you kissed.
That real special one.
You know, the one that you wished...wasn't...a cousin.
The one about the same age as you.
Grandma was always asking, "Where is them two?".

The cousin you slept on the floor with.
In the bed head to feet.
You wore each others clothes
and
their nickname was 'Skeet'.
Y'all fought over toys, the TV and who would sit in front.
Who would be Michael Jackson
and
who threw the first punch.
The cousin whose kids made you feel more like an uncle or aunt
The cousin that hooked you up
and got you a job at the plant.

Cousins
Glad I got 'em.
Aint' nothing like them.

To all my cousins,
Much love.

Hot Sauce

Can you imagine a world without spices?
No salt or pepper or no garlic.
Oreganos, sugars, currys and herbs
But could you imagine no hot sauce in the world?
That tangy, yangy, spicy, smack your lips,
Breath in deep,
Lick your finger tips.
Head sweats and eyes water,
Clear your nose and curl your toes.
That hot sensation .
That zing and zap.
If it don't taste good,
Hot sauce will take care of that.

You can put it on...

smothered potatoes
fried green tomatoes.

green beans
pinto beans
kidney beans.

red beans
navy beans
black beans
rice.

chicken....baked
barbecued or
fried.

chitt'lin's
ribs
pork chops
What?
Hot sauce will work it out.
Trust.

turnip greens
collard greens
mustard or mixed.

filet
whiting
perch
or cat fish.

pig feet...boiled
pig feet...pickled or
pig feet...still attached to the
ankle.

spinach
broccoli
spahghetti
chilli.

corn
tacos
shrimp.

Not just a dash.
Pour it on.
Don't skimp.

Tabasco sauce?
Not!!!
It's got to be Red Hot.

WHAT DOES IT REALLY MATTER

What does it really matter,
If I'm late for work?
My bills are late
Like they always are.
Went to the ATM and didn't no money come out.
Visa got rejected
And another check bounced.
But that's OK
Cause I made it through yesterday.
Thirteen more minutes and this one's history.
If I made it through all the other shit,
Why not this?
Why should I quit?

There are so many more important things in this life.
I want my mansion, my baby and my wife.
I can handle what this world throws at me.
Just let me be me.
Just let me be free.

What does it really matter,
If I drink too much?
That's just your opinion.
At least I takes my ass to work.
And sometimes I might exaggerate the truth.
I think I know it all.
And I fucked up my youth.
But these things,
In the big picture, ain't deep.
Cause above it all,
I 've got peace.
I'm free at least.

What does it really matter?
Cause it really ain't that deep.
What does it really matter?
I can't loose no sleep.
What does it really matter?
At least I got peace.
Anyway, it's all about...
What works for me.

Traveler

I've traveled close to heaven and throughout space.
Soared across the galaxies but none like this place.
It has awesome capabilities.
Ways to work things out.
Enormous responsibilities.
How is it possible?
Have you ever thought?
Where does that force come from?
From below or from above.
From within or
From love.

I've never been to a place like this.
It's truly one of a kind.
Unique and fresh.
It has it's own frequency.
It's own space and time.
The New York of the galaxy.
A guardian angels' fantasy,
To live among humanity.
Thanks for the journey.
Trust me.
I'll be back next century.

CHAPTER TWO

Natural Phenomenom

I LOVE HIS DIRTY DRAWZ

WHILE I WAS CLEANING THE ROOM
I PICKED UP HIS SHIRT.
IT SMELLED LIKE HIS COLOGNE.
I WANTED TO CALL HIM AT HOME.
I PICKED UP THE PHONE
BUT HE WAS GONE.

WONDERED WHERE HE WAS AT.
BUT DIDN'T HAVE TO WORRY ABOUT THAT.

BECAUSE...

I LOVE HIS DIRTY DRAWZ
CAUSE THEY SMELL SO GOOD.
I'D DO ANYTHING FOR HIM.
YES... I WOULD.

HE LOOKS GOOD AND
IS GOOD.
FEELS GOOD TOO.
HE TASTES GOOD.
TREATS ME GOOD.
HE'S MY BOO.

I LOVE HIS DIRTY DRAWS
CAUSE THEY SMELL SO NICE.
I LOVE HIS DIRTY DRAWZ
AND HE LUVS MINE.

THE DYNAMIC DUO

WE ARE LIKE THE DYNAMIC DUO

BATMAN AND ROBIN

OR

FRED AND BARNEY

L.A. AND BABYFACE

LEWIS AND MARTIN

TOM AND JERRY

FRANKIE AND JOHNNY

THELMA AND LOUISE

AMOS AND ANDY

CAPTAIN AND TENNIELE

SONNY AND CHER

MALCOLM AND MARTIN

SALT AND PEPPER

PEANUT BUTTER AND JELLY

A.T. AND T.

LIGHT AND DARK

UP AND DOWN

HIP AND HOP

IN AND OUT

MARQUE AND CHARLES

You've Taken Me Places

You've taken me places
that the Starship Enterprise can't go.
You've taken me places
that the Starship Enterprise can't go.
Destinations and journeys
that only you and I know.

First class accommodations.
Galactic conversation.
I'll be the passenger
and you can be the captain.

Why don't we cruise on warp speed?
Make a stop at the next galaxy.
No other passengers can go
'cause this is a private show.

You've taken me places
that the Starship Enterprise can't go.
No time machine
or Space shuttle.
You've taken me places
that the Starship Enterprise can't go.
Destinations and journeys
that only you and I know.

He is...

realer
wiser
sharper
quick.
finer
funnier
still kicks it.
spiritual
intellectual
and will check you.
breaks it down
ain't shit he won't do.
a real down brother
"why ya'll bull shit'n'?"
forget the past.
let's make this happen.
superstar stylist.
universes' finest.
my man
my niggah
my boo...

my you.

HERE

I WISH HE COULD BE HERE.
I WISH HE WAS NEAR.
HIS ARMS AROUND ME.
HIS BREATH IN MY EAR.

LAST NIGHT IT WAS ON.
INTENSE.
IT WAS DEEP.
WE MADE STUPID CRAZY LOVE
THAT CAME FROM ABOVE.

WE WENT PLACES THAT AN AIRPLANE CAN'T GO.
NOT EVEN THE SPACE SHUTTLE?
NO!
AND THE STARSHIP ENTERPRISE
COULDN'T GIVE US A RIDE
ESPECIALLY ON THAT KIND OF HIGH.

ELECTRICITY PULSED THROUGH US
WHEREVER SKIN CAME TO TOUCH.
IT WAS ALMOST TOO MUCH.
A MAJOR HEAD RUSH.

I WISH HE COULD BE HERE.

NEAR.

I WISH HE WAS HERE.
HIS ARMS AROUND ME
HIS BREATH IN MY EAR.

I'd Rather

I'd rather love him
than hate him.
I'd rather kiss him
than kill him.
I'd rather rub him
than wrong him.
I'd rather hold him
than harm him.

I'll trust him
not trick him.
I'll love him and
not loath him.

I'd rather smile at him
than spit at him.
I'd rather comfort him
than curse him.
I'd rather reach him
than ruin him.
choose him
than loose him.

I'd bear any of his pain
and he would do the same.

THE LONGEST TIME WE WERE APART

THE LONGEST TIME WE WERE APART
WAS THE LONGEST TIME
WITHOUT YOUR TOUCH.
NOT SEEING YOUR FACE AND
NOT HEARING YOUR VOICE.

BUT I HAD LAST NIGHTS' MEMORIES.
RIGHT BEFORE I LEFT.
IT WAS 'DA BOMB.
WE COULDN'T HELP OURSELVES.
WHILE I WAS GONE
EVERY LOVE SONG
SUNG BY DONNELL JONES
WAS ABOUT US.
EVERY REVELATION.
EACH NEW SENSATION.
ANOTHER INSPIRATION
SHARED WITH YOU.

THINKING ABOUT WHEN TO CALL YOU.
IT'S EARLY THERE
DON'T WANT TO WAKE YOU.

THE LONGEST TIME WE WERE APART
I COULDN'T WAIT TO TELL YOU.
I COULDN'T WAIT TO SHOW YOU.
I COULDN'T WAIT TO HOLD YOU.

I LIKE THE WAY

I LIKE THE WAY YOU SQUEEZE MY WAIST.
I LIKE THE WAY YOU SAY I TASTE.
I AM THE BUTTER AND YOU ARE THE BISCUIT.
PLEASE DON'T QUIT.
CAUSE I WON'T QUIT.

MY LOVE .
YOUR LOVE.
OUR LOVE .
IN LOVE.
FEEL YOU.
TASTE YOU.
AWE YOU.
LOVE YOU.

I LIKE THE WAY YOU SAY A WORD.
I LIKE THE WAY THAT YOU ARE CURVED.
I LIKE THE WAY YOU MAKE ME FEEL.
I LIKE YOU BEING REAL.

MY MAN.
MY NIGGAH.
MY BOY.
MY HOMMIE.
BUTTERSCOTCH MANDINGO.
SIGNIFICANT OTHER.
ACE.
BOOM.
KOON.
PARTNER.
SOUL MATE
LOVER.

OOMPH!... OOMPH!...OOMPH!
YOU AND ME.
US AND WE.
YOU...MY BABY.
NO...YOU... MY... BABY.

WHAT AM I GON' DO WITH YOU?
JUST LOVE ME AND BE TRUE.

Over and Over

I fall in love with you
over and over.
Each day I find more
of you to discover.
So glad that you
are my lover.
Can't imagine living this life with out you
or with another.

It took a bad past to get to this future.
I'd do it again because you were worth it.
It's amazing how life can reward you
above and beyond how you could imagine it.

Can't imagine my life if you were not in it.
You are a tough act to follow.
Don't want this to end.
The depth of my love I hope you know.
Cause baby you're the one that steals the show.

You are a dream come true
but better than I could have imagined.
I always believed
that there really was magic.
An eternity with you
I plan to spend.
And in this love story...
there is no end.

NATURAL PHENOMENON

When I first met you,
it was love
when you spoke.
It was no joke
and it scared me so.
I knew you were my one,
my two
and my three.
Our souls connected
Our spirits.
Harmony.
I could not believe
that this was real.
I was finally rescued
So glad I met you.
Love hit me like an earthquake,
a hurricane,
and a thunderstorm.
a major catastrophe,
all rolled into one.
On that night I knew
my search for love was finally done.
You hit me like
a monsoon,
a volcano and the bright morning sun.
Me and you boo.
A natural phenomenon.
You're my yin and I'm your yang.
What we got is hard to understand.
It's not common to have a love like this.
Look at the statistics.
Love is a guaranteed risk.
But I love you so
and you always show
that your love is...
just as equal.
It was like El Nino,
an avalanche and
mud slide.
The way you touched my soul
down deep inside.
It was like a meteor,
a comet and
the Big Bang.
When my eyes met yours,
I knew my life would change.
Fate took over
and life would never be the same.
You became
My soul mate.
My friend.
God... I don't want this to end.

CHAPTER THREE

Drama

End of An Adventure

Crack took another one of my men
and this time we can make it short and sweet.
It's over.
The end.
No... "Baby I'm sorry."
"I'll never do it again."
"But, why did you?"
"I don't know...why...
it just... happened."

I should have left your ass the first time you admitted
That you even
used that shit.
But, you weren't gon' do it no more.
Said, "I'm through."
"I quit."
No..."Baby I love you."
No..."We can get through this."
"We can work this out."
"Fuck that shit !!!"

I thought you were different.
My true soul mate.
But I started to see signs;
some flaws... some weakness.
My fantasy was tarnished.
I did not look at you the same.
I really really thought... you were
that perfect man.

You first stayed out... late... one night.
Then you lied about
where you were at.
This was way out of character.
Then you admitted that you smoked crack.

"But at least I told you", you said.
But, I had been through before.
How could you of all people go there?
You just don't know how much that hurt.
I don't like these feelings
because I am feeling your drama.
And I know you'll be all right.
I'm just sorry it's over.

I thought you were the one
I'd spend my old age with.
And I had said that before.
But you were for sure.
You brought euphoria to my life.
We saw the corners of the world.
You told me it was mine
but you did not have your own.

Can you survive with out me?
That's really the irony.
Prove me wrong.
Will you...please?

I am mad as hell with you.
I can't believe you went there.
This...?
I never would have thought.
It's the end of an adventure.

I'm numb.
I can't think.
I can't sit still
Is this real?

The ultimate betrayal
to the one who gave you all.
I am sure I will get over it.
But, shit...!
I'm in shock.

Am I sorry I met you?
Hell no.
It was all good.
It's just the end of our adventure.
The end of this show.

Divorce Party

An old friend and I met at a hotel in New York.
This time... we were both getting divorced.
Didn't do shit,
Just chilled.
Had a few drinks.
And our guts started to spill.
Boo...ed and hoo...ed...
And then we got mad.
Only for a moment
And then back to sad.
Talked about old times and our past.
How we...use to be... and how... "shit don't last."
Said we would be alone forever.
Fall in love again?...
NEVER!
Said we'd never go through that pain.
But what's really ashame...

We said that same shit the last time.

Not Over That

I ain't leaving you no matter what.
There is nothing you can do to make me leave you.
You are far more precious than that.
I love you times ten.
I love you to no end.
I'll love you until life does not exist,
Till the sun shines no more,
DNA deep and
Spirit to spirit.
I'll love you until
Grass is not green and when day is not light.
I still ain't leaving you,
Not after last night.

What would I do without you?
I'd only still think of you all of the time.
Is he gonna call?
Is he in someone elses' arms.
What if I see him out?
How should I act ?
I don't want to go through that.

Because you are the one for me.
The only place my soul feels free.
I don't want to be alone on this journey.
So don't you see...
I would not leave you over that.
As a matter of fact, I've done worse than that.

So baby please don't beat yourself.
I love you more than I love myself.
I don't want to see you in pain.
Let's get through this and on to the next phase.
I love you so and I don't want you to go.
Don't know what I'd do if you walked out.
The test of love is what this is about.

All is forgiven.

Scorned Woman

A scorned woman ain't no joke.
There's a hot sauce named after her
called...
Inferno.
And to handle her can be a nuclear hell.
She'll never trust you and she won't forget
how you were bold enough to hold
another and get caught.
Stand back.
Take cover.
She's boiling.
She's hot.

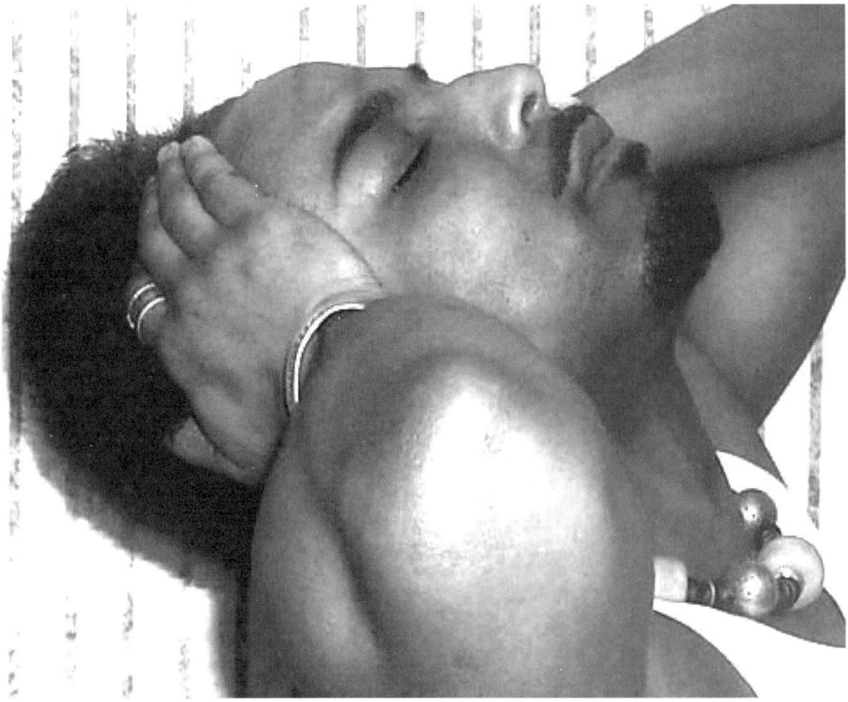

PAIN

PAIN.
PAIN.
GO AWAY.
YOU BETTER COME BACK ON YESTERDAY.
PAIN.
PAIN.
PAIN.
WHY'D YOU COME BY?
I HURT SO BAD AND
I JUST WANT TO CRY.

PAIN ...PAIN ...PAIN.
WHY'D YOU EVEN CALL?
I'VE ALREADY BEEN THERE.
CAN'T GO BACK.
THAT'S ALL.

I FELT LIKE THERE WAS A RIP IN MY SOUL.
A HURT SO DEEP AND I COULD NOT LET GO.
IF OTHERS CAN MAKE IT,
WHY NOT ME TOO?
SO I'VE MADE UP IN MY MIND
THAT'S WHAT I'M GOING TO DO.

SO...
PAIN...
PAIN ...
PAIN...
PAIN...
PAIN.
GO AWAY.
MATTER A FACT,
DON'T EVEN COME MY WAY.
PAIN............PAIN.......PAIN
I WON'T FEEL IT AGAIN.
I'VE DONE MY TIME AND
YOU'RE NOT MY FRIEND.

BUT... PAIN ...PAIN...PLEASE....!
JUST GIVE ME PEACE.
I CAN'T TAKE IT AND I NEED A RELEASE.
SO ...PAIN
DON'T STOP BY.
DON'T EVEN WRITE.
BECAUSE YOU AIN'T WELCOME
WHEN YOU LEAVE THIS TIME.

THE GAME

HE GAVE YOU ATTENTION BUT
HE WAS ON A MISSION.
YOU TOOK THE PLUNGE.
AND HE WAS TOO YOUNG.
YOU WERE TOO LONELY AND
THAT LUST TURNED TO LOVE.

YOU FORGOT HOW THE GAME WAS PLAYED.
YOU WERE LOST.
YOU WERE INSANE.
AND HERE COMES THAT PAIN.
YOU SAID IT WOULDN'T HAPPEN AGAIN.

HE PLAYED YOU
BUT YOU PAID.
FOUND OUT HE LIKES TO SLEEP ALL DAY.
COMES THE NIGHT
HE SLIPS AWAY
AND THEN
DIDN'T SHOW UP ONE DAY.
YOU DIDN'T WANNA HEAR WHAT HE HAD TO SAY
THAT WAS UNTIL,
YOU SAW HIS FACE.
ALL DISCRETIONS WERE FORGOTTEN.
HIS EXPLANATION SEEMED VALID.

YOU FORGOT HOW THE GAME WAS PLAYED.
YOU WERE LOST,
YOU WERE INSANE,
AND HERE COMES THAT PAIN.
SAID IT WOULDN'T HAPPEN AGAIN.

WHAT WAS YOUR FIRST CLUE

WHAT WAS YOUR FIRST CLUE?
WHO PICKED UP WHO?
WHO PAID FOR THE DATE?
WHOSE HOUSE DID YOU GO TO?
WHO FELL IN LOVE FIRST?
WHO NEVER WENT TO WORK?
WHEN DID THEY MOVE IN?
NOW THEY HAVE YOUR PIN.

WHAT WAS YOUR FIRST CLUE?
THAT IT WASN'T GOING TO WORK
WHAT WAS YOUR FIRST CLUE?
YOU DO ALL THE WORK.

WATCH OUT FOR WHAT YOU DO.
CAN'T ALWAYS BE A FOOL.
THERE'S ALWAYS A FIRST CLUE
WE DON'T PAY ATTENTION TO.
WE BECOME BLIND TO THE FACT.
DON'T SEE THE REAL DEAL.
UNTIL WE'RE STUPID AND IN LOVE
AND THE DRAMA IS REVEALED.

WHERE DO THEY LIVE?
WHERE DO THEY WORK?
HOW DO THEY PAY THEIR BILLS?
DO THEY GO TO CHURCH?
DO THEY LOVE THEIR MAMMA?
HOW IS THEIR CREDIT?
HAVE A CRIMINAL RECORD???
AND ARE THEY IN DEBT?
HOW ARE THEY WITH KIDS?
HOW ARE THEY DRESSED?
HOW ARE THEIR SPIRITS?
AND DO THEY TAKE CARE OF THEMSELF?

PAY ATTENTION TO WHAT YOUR GETTING.
IT ONLY TAKES 30 SECONDS.
THERE IS ALWAYS A FIRST CLUE.
BUT YOU'VE GOT TO DO YOUR INTERVIEW?

Lightening Was Bright

We took a walk through the hood last night.
Saw all our old familiar spots.
Fourth of July fireworks display,
block barbecues and hanging by the lake.
Reminisced about all the fun we had.
We would be the two who would last,
The ones to stick it out
and show what love's about.

Then came the storm
early the next morn.
And the lightning was bright.
Almost took out my sight.
So hard to recover.
I hope I get over.
How could you do something so cruel?
I'll love you forever
Can't believe we're through.

I tried to figure out what went wrong.
Agonized.
All day long.
Played all the scenes over in my head.
Tried to remember what was said.
Was it this
Or
Was it that?
Did I get all the facts?
I can't believe this has happened to us.
Or is this kind of love doomed from birth.

WHY DOES LOVE MAKE YOU ACT LIKE THIS

Why does love make you act like this?
Broke my car windows,
Cussed,
Fought and spit.
You do things
You know you shouldn't
Like calling my job and
Hiding behind bushes.
Is it really love making you act like a fool?
You bleached my clothes.
You're breaking all the rules.
Why does love make you act this?
Have you cutting car tires
And setting houses on fire.
Is it love
Or is it crazy?
Drank too much or
Insecure... maybe?
You say it's love that makes you fatal attract.
Cause this last attack,
Sure won't get me back.
You call and hang the phone
Just to see if I'm at home.
Everytime I'd get a beep,
You'd call the numbers when I was sleep.
So get off that chandelier
And let me make this real clear.
You are not in love.
You are just crazy.
I can't be with you
Because you really do scare me.
You call this love.
But I don't think so.
You are out cold.
And I gotta go.
Why does love make you act like this?
Your passions turned to vengeance.
Who would of thought that it would have come to this.
That's not love making you act like this.

all i did was wished it

all i did was wished it and it came true.
all i did was wished it and in stepped you.
all i ever wished for
and everything i asked.
you were the one i thought would last.
renaissance man.
real first class.
charming and sensitive
and you made me laugh.

we were gonna get old together and
see the rest of the world.
we both loved life
and wanted to taste more.
i loved you deep
but then you changed.
something went wrong.
you did not act the same.
they say with love
there always comes some pain.
but i had asked for... you.
i just don't know what happened.

CHAPTER FOUR

In Between

LOVE ME SOME HIM

I love me some him
because his love is like no other.
It's not the same as hers.
He's a friend,
a partner and lover.

We connect on a lot of levels.
Mind body and soul.
We've got a "stand out" love.
Everybody can tell.

I love me some him
and I feel free to say it.
And I love her too,
it 's just not the same.

She had my child.
The woman I chose.
Just how special she is,
I don't think she knows.

We can work this out.
We can get through,
Since it has been discovered,
This love I have for two.
She has her own place in my heart
and he does too.
She'll always be my girl.
but he's gon' be my boo.

It's All the Same

Steven had Gene
who had Stanley
who had me
who had Charles
who had him and her.

Jackie ate Debra
who was stuck by Drew
who was sucked by Lou...ooh.

I want him.
he wants her.
she wants two at the same time.
he wants me
so does she
lust..
it's all the same.

DO YOU...TOO?

I do and I don't.
I will or I won't.
I want you.
I want to.
Do you...too?

Would it be wrong or right?
I don't like this fight.
But I want to.
Do you... too?

Your hers' and he's mine.
I'm no good at lies .
I don't know
what to
do.

Had the chance way back when
but, you were with my best friend.
I said no.
You said, "What for?"
but...you know.

I do and I don't.
I will or I won't .
I want you.
I want to.
Do you too?

You called me last night.
Said you'd be on the next flight.
We got past the wrong and the right.
So for just this one night,
Let's enjoy the time.
I know you love your wife.
I am not trying to mess up your life.
But I want you.
I want to.
Do you...too?

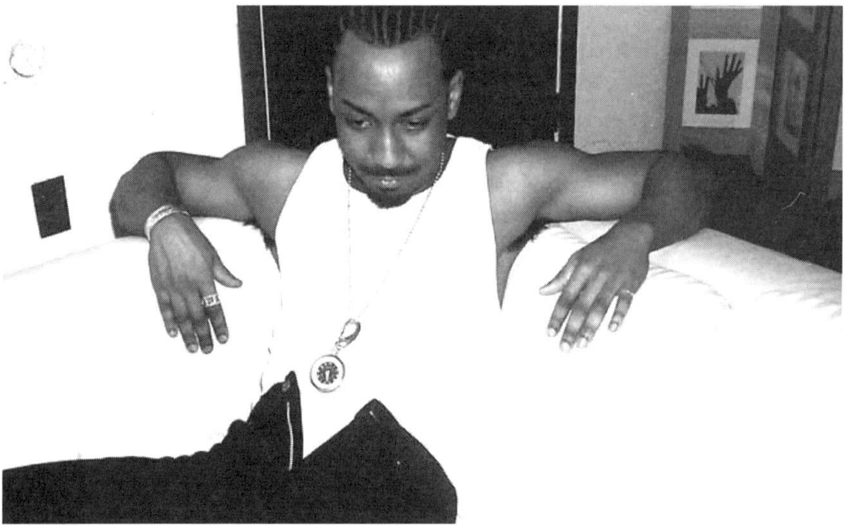

What's Wrong with This Picture

What's wrong with this picture?
He's gooked me and you.
What's wrong with this picture?
I ain't trying to be no fool.

I ain't mad at you girl.
Cause he's got it like that.
You got his kids.
And I ain't got shit.
Wasn't trying to break up your thang.
But I really didn't know,
He had a wife and another life
And I was just the 'ho'.

What's wrong with this picture?
He fooled me and you too.
What's wrong with this picture..?
Is that I got better things to do.

I'm not fighting you over him.
I'll chalk it up as experience .
I am not going out cussing and pointing fingers.
And you won't catch me on Jerry Springer.
It was too good to be true.
But I have some good advice for you.
Get free of that black voodoo.
He's not through and we're not the only two.

He...This and Her...That.

I love them both for the things they give.
It's just the way it is.
I love them both for what they bring to the table.
What one can't do, the other is able.

he lust.
her life.
her trust.
his time.

he lies.
she trips.
he can't come by.
she flips the script.

him is hot.
her is tight.
him like it a lot.
her like it on top.

him smooth.
her cool.
him real.
her moods.

he and me.
me and she.
the best of both worlds.
fantasy
and
reality.

I'm Sho' Is

I'm sho is
gon' get my hair did.
he be my man for life
cause I'm carrying his chil'
you just a booty call
girlfriend...
that's all.

get real.

I'm sho is.
gon' get my hair did.
we gon' get back together.
we gots a strong relationship.

he still sleeping with me
and... also miss thing
you need 2 know...
he's the babys' daddy.

did he say he loved you?
well he told me that too.
did he love you all night and
promise you the moon?

give it up girl.
this ain't cute.
have some respect for yourself.
don't look like a fool.

I'm sho is.
gon' get my hair did.
I'm still his.
and you can't win.

I'm sho is.
gon' get my hair did.
gon' be his.
till the end of this life
get it right
you his ho'
but...
I'm his wife.

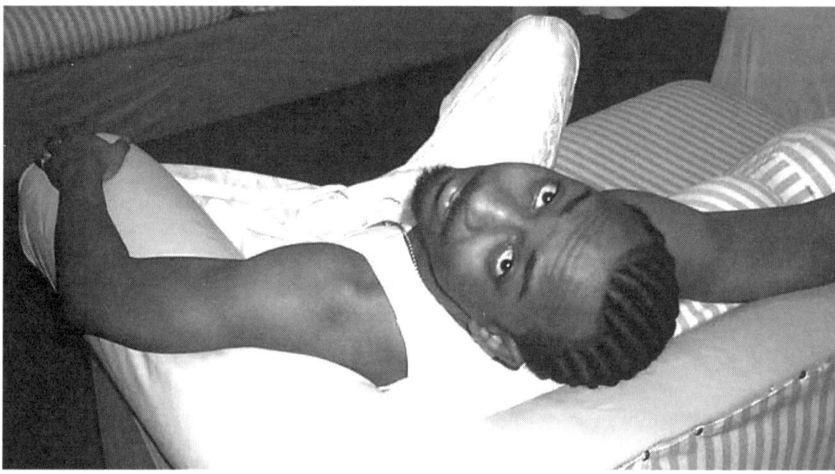

In Between

in between
a unique place to be.
in between
a love for he and she.
in between
the best of both worlds.
in between
I know it can work.

what about
what the people might say?
what about
whose time... which one today?
what about
if it's wrong or right?
what about
Me living... my life.

in between
gives a new perspective.
in between
gives a new respect.
in between
is not black or white.
in between
is not wrong or right.
been going on since
the dawn of time.

CHAPTER FIVE

No...Love

"No weapon formed against me shall prosper."

Dear Pastor,

I attended your so called "Family Day"
last Sunday.
I did not like what you had to say
about those labeled 'gay'.
You went totally Hollywood.
That day I vowed I never would
attend your church ever again.
I am sick of that message.
Praise the lord ,
amen.

I'd rather be the way I am and honorable,
than the way you are and not.
Take a look in the mirror just in case you forgot.

For I am
a Strong, Black and Proud man.
I am spiritual and intellectual.
Responsible and respectful.
Educated and dedicated
Creative and talented
I am world traveled,
well adjusted,
stress free
and healthy.
Accomplished.
Honored
and priviledged.
Prosperous beyond what I could ask or think.
I am loving and well loved.

I am happy and living in 'Heaven' on this Earth.

I am all these things
but...
I am not... as you so tackily put it...no Sissy!

COMMON

IT'S COMMON TO DRINK COFFEE IN THE MORNING WITH
ORANGE JUICE A BAGEL AND THEN COMMUTE TO WORK.
PUNCHING IN 9 TO 5
WEEK AFTER WEEK.
DAY AFTER DAY.

IT'S COMMON TO SMOKE AFTER A MEAL.
EAT LUNCH AT 12.
DINNER AT 8.
COUNTING CALORIES
AND TRYING TO LOOSE WEIGHT.

IT'S COMMON TO GO TO FLORIDA FOR THE WINTER.
BLUE JEANS
T-SHIRTS AND
JOINING A GYM.

COMMON.

TENNIS SHOES
CHURCH EVERY SUNDAY
HAMBURGERS AND FRENCH FRIES
BASEBALL HATS
BUISNESS SUITES AND TIES.

COMMON.

THEY ALWAYS SAY YOU ARE TERRIBLE AT TWO,
WHICH THE RECORD SHOWS IS DEFINITELY TRUE.
WE START SCHOOL IN KINDERGARTEN
THEN 12 YEARS OF GRAMMAR
YOU ARE GROWN AT 18
AT 21 YOU CAN DRINK.
4 YEARS OF COLLEGE
THEN NO JOB
IS COMMON.

SHOULD BE MARRIED BY 25
YOU'RE OLD OVER 30
50 IS MID-LIFE
AND YOU SHOULD BE SURPRISED
IF AT 90 YOU'RE STILL ALIVE.

COMPLAINING OF ONE'S HEALTH
AND NOT THINKING FOR ONE'S SELF.

COMMON.

BE UNIQUE
MAKE YOU OWN PATH
TRAVEL YOUR OWN JOURNEY.
DO SOMETHING DIFFERENT.
BREAK AWAY FROM
COMMON.

KNOW US

They don't understand us.
(and now it seems they want to know).
We know almost every thing about them,
But they don't know us.

We know their hair.
We know their ways,
We know their talk,
And a lot of times their thought.

Why?
Brainwashed.

We know almost everything about them,
But they don't know us.

You know you steal !
You know you cheat !
You know you lie !
You know you rape !
You twist the truth.
Hide the truth.
And falsely acclaim.
We know the game
And you ain't ashamed.
And yet, you continue to do the same.

We know everything about you,
But you don't know us.

Talk to your ancestors and they will tell you
Our magnificent and great story and
Of all the sons and daughters
That became their slaughter.

They'll tell you of mighty black men
And great nations of people
Of whom, we are the sons and daughters.

Today's ***new*** *slaughter.*

See...we talk to our ancestors and they talk to us.
They've told us of our life before our forced exodus.
You see... we... know everything about us
Despite you not wanting us to know.
But 500 years of oppression is long over due.
We'll use your rules.
The way you taught us to.
We'll even play your game,
Don't be surprised if ours' is the same.
See...we know everything about y'all.
But y'all don't know "shit" about us.

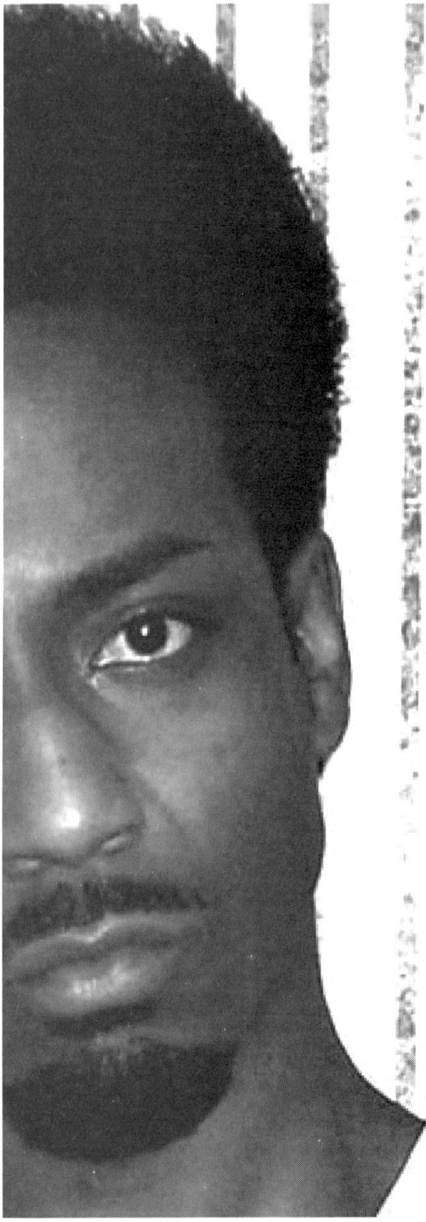

No...Love I

If you were black
and I was white,
the things you did to me,
I would not have done to you.

If you were poor
and I was rich,
there is nothing
I would not give you.

If I was stronger
and you were weaker,
I'd spread my hands
to help and heal you.

But because I have loved
and you have hated,
I have got
no...love...
for you.

No Love II

They gave us no love
the day my father died.
Mom got stopped
following the ambulance from behind.
Told them she was speeding because
dad was having pains in his chest.
But that didn't matter,
she still got the ticket.
They had no heart.
I could not believe it.

They gave her no love.
They gave us no love.

A colleague said I should not be here.
The day my daddy died.
I should have went home
and I wasn't acting like
he was gone.
She gave me no love.
Showed no remorse.
How could she be so cold,
malicious and bold?

They took my man to jail.
Got the money for bail.
Gets up to the door.
They tell me it's more.
They showed us no love.
Showed no remorse.
But that's OK because
retribution is going to come
One hour, one day.
If there's a God,
they'll pay.

They showed my people no love
the day my daddy died.
They showed us no love.
But that's all right
vengance is nigh.

We were...

enslaved
stolen
abused
prejudged
refused
disrespected
rejected
tormented
beaten
lied on
spit on
stepped on
lynched
crucified
drowned
cut
shot
and bound
dismembered
disfigured
disadvantaged
diminished
harassed
provoked
peeved
disgraced
humiliated
shamed
demeaned
defiled
cursed
damned
dissed
criticized
ostracized
brutalized
tireless
indefatigable

copied
yearning
grieving
worshipped
adored
revered
idolized
lauded
praised
exalted
victors
champions
victors
resilient
rare
unprecedented
deadly
fierce
immortal.

CHAPTER SIX

Ooh!...aah!

ANATOMY OF AN ORGASM
(The Highest Form of Physical Pleasure)

*THE LOOK...OOH
THE LUST...UMMM
DESIRE TO TOUCH
AAAH!... OOMPH!.... OOMPH!
OOOH!....AAAH!
OUCH BABY...NOT SO HARD!
HOT
HEAT
INTENSE
ELECTRIC.
SUCK
ROLL
RUB
AND LICK.
MOAN AND GROAN
BUMP AND GRIND
BACK THAT THANG ON IT.
BUMP
SMACK
SMELL
TASTE.
BITE IT
SQUEEZE THAT WAIST.
TIGHT
THROBBING
PULSATING
GRIPPING
SQUEEZING
HEAVY BREATHING.
"IT'S COMING ...BABY!"
(NO NAMES JUST...BABY)
GOING HIGHER AND HIGHER AND HIGHER AND
UNGH...UNGH...UNGH...SSSSSSS!!
then...BOOOOM!!!
THE EXPLOSION!!!
UNGH...UNGH...UNGH...UNGH...AAAH...YEAH
THE FIREWORKS!
UNGH...OOOH
FLOODING!
HEAD RUSH!
BLACKOUT.
ALMOST NEAR DEATH EXPERIENCE .
BOOM! BAM! BOOM! BOOM!
BOOM!... BOOM! BOOM!
BOOM!.. BOOM!
BOOM!
SENSITIVE OOOH...SSSSSSS...AAAH
DELICATE...AAAH
WARM...UMMM
RELEASE.
RELIEF.*

*AGAIN?
YEAH WHEN?
GIVE ME ABOUT TEN.*

Freakery

*I likes the freak-er-ee.
I likes the freak-er-ee.
I likes the freak-er-ee.
Because it's all in me.*

*Welcome
to the freak factory.
It's better than
the fantasy.*

*It's all in my bones.
I've got to get my Jones.
You are welcome.
Big fun so come.*

*Now if you feel me
on the freak-er-ee,
we got to get off.
Doggy style
or you on top.
By myself or
with help.*

*Slap it,
rub it,
flip it down.
Make sure its clean.
and don't forget the towel.*

HO'

NEGRESS
GODDESS
EMPRESS
LADY

LIONESS
HEIRESS
TRAMP

STEWARDESS
WAITRESS
ACTRESS

BARONESS
PRINCESS
VAMP

COUNTESS
MISTRESS
WIDOW

MISS THING
DIVA
HO'

ELEMENTS OF LOVE

PASSION
LUST
TRUST.

LOVE OF "THE FREAK ON"
AND GOOD RHYTHM
A MUST.

ELECTRICITY
HARMONY
SENSITIVITY.

SOME CLEAN SHEETS
AND A WHOLE LOT OF CREATIVITY.

Up with the Vampires

Up with the vampires~
Got my creep on all night.
Looking for a victim.
Standing in dim light.
Looking for love.
No blood.
It's tight.
Wondering if
This is wrong or right.
I should be sleep like everyone else
But when the hunger comes,
I can't help myself.

Up with the vampires
And it's really a fight.
Picking cotton
On a 13 hour flight.
Found no love.
No blood.
It's tight.

Up with the vampires
And here comes the light.
Back to the coffin.
But hold up...now... love's in sight.
Another victim to the game.
No need for a name.
They're all the same.

Up with the vampires
And here comes the light.
Gotta dash.
Gotta go.
Losing that shadow.

I'll be back when it's tight.
In the last hours of a night.
Looking for love.
Whether wrong or right?

NONSTOP

LOOK AT THE GLOBE AND CHOOSE, BABY,
ANYWHERE YOU WANT TO GO.
NONSTOP TO ANY DESTINATION BABY
FIRST CLASS
LET'S ROLL.

IS IT HARD TO CHOOSE?
PICK A PLACE.
YOU CAN'T LOOSE.
YOU CAN VISIT THEM ALL.
LET ME MAKE A QUICK CALL.

I'LL TAKE YOU ANYWHERE IN THE UNIVERSE.
YOU DON'T NEED ANY CREDIT CARDS.
EAST OR WEST?
WHICH WAY FIRST?
EUROPE OR THE ISLANDS?
MARS OR VENUS?
ACTUALLY, BABY,
WE DON'T HAVE TO GO ANYWHERE.
WE CAN JUST STAY IN.

BUT WE'RE STILL GOING SOMEWHERE
NONSTOP TO OUR DESTINATION.

"But
He
Could
Throw
Down."

BUT... HE COULD THROW DOWN

NO JOB.
NO CAR.
NO PLACE TO STAY.
ONE OR MORE BABIES.
IT'S REALLY HARD TO SAY.
HE LIKES TO PLAY ALL KIND OF WAYS.
IT JUST DEPENDS ON WHOSE SPONSORING THAT DAY.

KNOWS HOW TO PULL THAT HAIR
AND TALK SHIT IN YOUR EAR.
WILL FREAK YOU OUT.
MAKE YOU TALK ABOUT.

IT'S KNOWN ALL OVER TOWN
THAT HE CAN THROW DOWN.
THE BROTHER IS KNOWN AS THE BEST LAY AROUND.

HE TREATS YOUR BABY REAL GOOD.
THIS BROTHER AIN'T NO FOOL.
USED HIS STAMPS TO BUY YOU FOOD
AND PICKED UP A 40 OUNCE TOO.
OH... THE MAN'S REAL COOL
AND SUSPICIOUSLY NICE
BUT WHEN YOU BREAK IT DOWN, IT'S ALL FOR A PRICE.

SECRET IS THAT HE LIKES THAT PIPE.
AND HAS BEEN KNOWN TO START A FIGHT.
DIDN'T COME HOME LAST NIGHT
AND THIS AIN'T THE FIRST TIME.
RIGHT?

BUT THAT'S WHAT HAPPENS WHEN YOU FALL FOR A ROCK STAR.
PASSION, DRAMA AND SHIT YOU COULDN'T THINK OF.
SO PACK THOSE BAGS AND CALL IT THE END
IS IT REALLY WORTH IT BECAUSE HE'S GOOD IN BED?

Grease On the Sheets

Grease on the sheets
and the pillow cases too.
Oh well, lay back an let's just continue.
These are the good sheets
and they can be washed out.
Freakin'
not neatness
is not what this is about.

Grease on the sheets.
We can change them later.
What's going on now is all that matters.
There was grease on them the last time
and there be grease on them the next time.
So in the meantime,
let's take our time
and finsh this grind.

Make me cum !!!
Then you can go!!!

CHAPTER SEVEN

Interview with JESUS

Tell Them

Tell them that he tried to kill you with car wrecks and diseases.
Tell them that he tried to possess you with evil spirits and demons.
Tell them he attacked your body
but you kept on praying.
Tell them you'd do it again.
"Well done,
my son,
Amen."

But I did not know what I was here to do.
But now... I do.
I just listened to your voice
and you guided me through.
And... yes... I would do it again
and you would not have to ask.
I am your son.
I was born for this task.

I will teach the people
of the freedom in you.
And to love thyself first is
Life's number one rule.

Black Voodoo

Black Voodoo
it can heal or hurt you.
Black Voodoo
it can help or harm you.
Black Voodoo
Ain't no joke.
Black Voodoo
I've warned.
I've spoke.

Black Voodoo
Given only to a few.
Don't ever cross one
with the gift of
The Roots.

Good and evil spirits
almost at your command.
Miracles and wonders
only you will understand.
Just never get mad
and raise your hand.
For if you do,...

You better mean it.

Santa Claus Is A Lie

Why do you lie to your child?
Tell them there's a... Santa Claus.
You say he'll come down the chimney.
He'll bring them toys and all for... free!
You live in a flat in the city.
Two bedrooms, one bath and... no chimney.

You want your child to be open with you but,
You did not start out with the truth.
They are raised with lies from age two.
Now as adults, they tell that lie too.
Santa Claus is a lie
and so untrue.
You should have told them
Santa Claus was... you.

Santa Claus is the biggest lie perpetrated
And every year you can't really afford it.
Christmas used to be about Christ.
It's commercialized and packaged.
The result of that lie.
Now you're caught in the game and
It's all for a price.

NEVER AGAIN

She'll miss her first roller coaster ride and kindergarten too.
She was just potty trained.
She was just two.
She'll never learn the latest dance or
Find love and true romance.
She'll never graduate from high school
Or go swimming in a pool.
She'll never say another word,
See the sun shine
Or chase a bird.
She'll never decorate a Christmas tree.
We will never know what she was to be.
She'll never have another birthday
Cause she died on Saturday.
Labor Day.
She was hit by a car
While playing at the park.
This girl in her youth.
This girl who was only two.
Was it because of this?
Or was it because of that.
It really does not matter
Because she is not coming back.
To the girl whose name I never knew,
I would have gladly traded places with you.

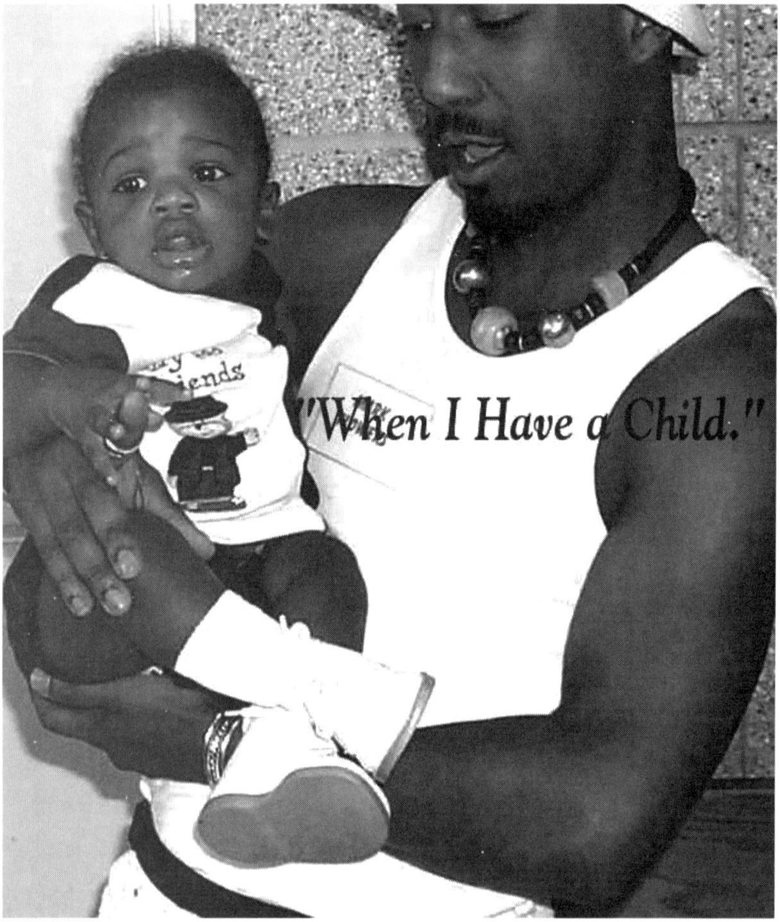
"When I Have a Child."

When I Have A Child

When I have a child there is so much I would say.
First... I love you so much.
So glad you came here.
This day.
My way.

Welcome to this world.
It's a crazy place.
So much to learn.
I hope I've paved your way.

I want your life to be even better than mine.
Love thyself first.
Learn much.
Please... take your time.
I can't wait till we have our first talk.
Till you roll over,
Crawl,
And walk.
I never want you to experience pain.
You will make mistakes
But that's part of this game.

And yes...
It's insane out here.
I just want you to be clear.
I'll give you all my all.
Live your life without fear.

You are flesh of my flesh
And bone of my bone.
Unconditional love for you
I will always show.

You could do no wrong
To make me stop loving you.
I'll always take care.
Be there.
When you need me to.

The Baby's Mama

I'm looking for the baby's mama.
A woman with true class and no drama.
Let me also mention the fact
She's got to be down and have my back.

A woman that's down with all of my shit.
If there is a challenge she can handle it.
She'll turn me on like no one's done before
She'll be the one I'd do anything for.
I've waited and searched for her for a long time.
She's got to be all that because competition is tight.
I'm taking my time until I find Mrs. Right.
She'll be spiritual, secure and have great style
And I'll want her to be the mother of my child.

We will marry
Make love and
concieve
our baby.

I hope our child has her qualities, strengths and characteristics
and I hope our child has my vision, creativity and love of great music.
Maybe she'll become the first woman President.
Maybe he'll cure cancer and discover new planets.

I'm looking for the baby's mamma.
I'm bringing my best to the table.
Her wish will be my command and
we'll be equal as woman and man.

Here's Why

If I should die
before you think its time.
Don't cry.
Please try.
Here's why.

If I should die
and you don't know why.
Please try,
Not to cry,
Here's why.

Had all my dreams come true
and found my soul mate too.
Been around the world.
Always had something to do.
The best of this
and the best of that.
Been there
done that.

So this is why.

If I should go
and you don't know why,
Don't cry.
Please try.
Here's why.

This world owes me nothing.
I did everything twice.
I've known a lot of people.
It's been a great life.
My journeys been better
than I could have imagined.
It's made me believe that there really is magic.

Had it all.
Had a ball.
Could not complain.
The hurt and pain.
The sun and rain.
Not a single thing
would I change.
I played my role.
My video.
If this I could pass,
live today like it's your last.

That's why.

Why Fear?

Fear even when it seems clear.
Fear of death and dying.
Wondering why is the baby crying.
Will I get to work late?
Will that last flight wait?
Will my bills be paid?

When will they get free?
When all around is need.
There is plenty for all
and to give it, is my dream.

If you can make time stand still,
Create life at will,
Cracked the mysteries of light
and then created flight,
Why can't they have what they need?

It's more possible than not.

Interview With JESUS

I met Jesus on a flight Christmas day.
He said, ***"That's not really my Birthday."***
I asked, "Well, what's up with all this greed?
Why are so many people in need?
I thought you died on the cross to set us free.
But there's still hunger, pain and poverty.
OK... can you at least hook it up
To where everyone has the basic needs;
Food, water and shelter?
and
How do you feel about ...how we... treat each other?
So what's heaven like and is God cooler than we think.
When I die, will I be caught up in the blink blink.
So... were you like a superstar?
And is everything OK so far?
Thanks for always having my back?
And can I tell all the folks you're Black.
Oh,
And will we be able to fly?
"Yes. and travel at the speed of light."
You gave your life to save all us
Even with all our madness?

Why?

How did you do it?
Did it hurt?
Did you know you were the Son of God?
Did you want more time?
Did at any point,
You want to change your mind?
Was it really hard?
Would you do it again?
When are you coming back?
And was it all worth it?"